DOROTHY PORTER

DRIVING
TOO FAST

ABOUT *UNTAPPED*

Most Australian books ever written have fallen out of print and become unavailable for purchase or loan from libraries. This includes important local and national histories, biographies and memoirs, beloved children's titles, and even winners of glittering literary prizes such as the Miles Franklin Literary Award.

Supported by funding from state and territory libraries, philanthropists and the Australian Research Council, *Untapped* is identifying Australia's culturally important lost books, digitising them, and promoting them to new generations of readers. As well as providing access to lost books and a new source of revenue for their writers, the *Untapped* collaboration is supporting new research into the economic value of authors' reversion rights and book promotion by libraries, and the relationship between library lending and digital book sales. The results will feed into public policy discussions about how we can better support Australian authors, readers and culture.

See untapped.org.au for more information, including a full list of project partners and rediscovered books.

Readers are reminded that these books are products of their time. Some may contain language or reflect views that might now be found offensive or inappropriate.

CONTENTS

I · IN EXTREMIS

CARMEN

Overture

Three days of heatwave,
A hot lid of dinning cicadas.
At night only a flock of bats lifts
    and flies across a hot scrap of moon.
Colours flow hot and slow like lava;
    the sea is never cold
    shining like the bluish basking belly
        of a snake.
Even mauve smoky twilight scratches along the skin
    behind the eyes
    like a hot thorn.
A black and white butterfly
    floats past a bright orange weed
        that flutters hungrily
            like a fly-trap.
Around an oozing broken pipe
    midges cluster
        ogling the milky water
            that gives off a green stink.
The road is empty
    but for the bright disturbing green feathers
        of a rainbow lorikeet
            smeared across the hot bitumen.

But. Look now.
There's a white light
        glancing off the water;
a spatter of rain
hisses on the road

and wafts up
    in a dew of dust and petrol;
flecks of parrot piss float
    from a luxuriant blossoming gum;
white cars
    in this fierce light
    hurt the most.
Carmen
    drives with one loose dark hand
Carmen
    drives a white hot car.

Carmen's Song

The swaying rainbow
    arched from the ocean to the lagoon,
my hands travel it
    like a lover's spine.
Together
    we move, we shift
    our light, our colours
        along the steaming road.
Are you
        in our way?

The rain will stop
the light will change
the trees will shine strangely
orange ... blue ... green ... red ... yellow
a shower of lollies or a bewitching?
Stand in my colours
with your eyes wide.

And see.

See your Carmen.

Under my rainbow's dome
we'll dance to each other's eyes
and entwine
like smitten cobras.

Dazzling as honeycomb
my rainbow is a snack,
    you can keep your balance
        your head
    on its delicious edge.

But
    remember
        I'm no sweet vapid stripe
        I'm Carmen
and I'll twine around your gut
    like a fishing line
        and I'll pull tight.

Don José's Song

You move fast
    beyond me
        like a nameless comet —

your fiery tail
    all ice
        lashes me in the face

but where you strike me
I am no longer desolate
I flower berserkly
    like a mountain after a spring flash-flood

my life is all balcony
    leaning out
    over a blue valley
    that allures like a clear, cold creek,
with you
    I leap off —

and spark
    no matter what I hit
    no matter what I break

Carmen, you're my white spider
    stabbing me with an elixir venom

you give me
    paralysis
you give me
    wings.

Carmen's Cards

My turn.
I have a knack with cards.
Through my fingers,
Poker. Tricks. I'm a fantastic cheat.
Or fortunes.
Let mine spread out.

Ace of spades.
The cards are sticking.
Again. The ace of spades.
Death. Always death.

This grubby card
    flashing up my road

like a storm's lightning mirror
when your own face flashes back
    from a black windscreen
        and gleams white —

I know a bit about death.
I know all about murder.

Passion is my murder.
I like my lovers
    to be
lunatics, show-offs, fools
    in a high trapeze act
swinging on Big Top sex
    and always working
        without a net.

They kill me.
They kill themselves.
Freedom is my murder.
Every hand
    tracing my face
every mouth
    guzzling my breast
becomes terrifying, silky
like a corpse's hair
and I recoil, jump barbed wire,
tear myself bloody
    to get free.

Don José has set himself on fire.
Lurching in tedious agony
    blaming, threatening me.

I am petrol, not water not a blanket.

Let him come, ace of spades,
    let him come.

Carmen's Finale

It's you.

You've arrived with the mosquitoes.

Here's my repellent.

I have nothing for you.
Time. Talk. Pity.
    Nothing.

Love's a rainforest after dark
    all dank, aromatic
        but you can't move for leeches.
I'm dreaming
   of a cool, free skin
     a white car
       all the windows down
          a night wind, an open road,
by myself.

no ferns. no phones.
no fire-flies. no hot eyes.

no stinging trees. no dagger tongues.
no leeches. no man's whine.

Just Carmen
   swept up
   in a high green sea wave —
Carmen —

transparent, tough,
   going-with-it
   like a sea-horse
over and over
   the salt water as familiar,
   as warm as my blood
crashing
   then spreading out
     in fine fierce foam.
That's Carmen. That's me.

Now.
   Piss off.

Don José's Knife

Gypsy eyes, wolf eyes.
Don't blink.

When the knife is a mirror
your face can't cut me.

Dance for me.
You're in danger.

Love's a wild eel.
I'll cut its head off.

Can you swim
against a knife river?

I'm very cold.
Just two colours.

There's troth.

There's death.

Don José's Finale

Your belly. Your blood all over me.

Carmen! *Carmen*

A black 'n' white abattoir. The light's gone.

Loss. A sea of petrol.

My burnt unloved hands. Are still wings.

I fly on black fire. For my dead witch.

OATES' DIARY

for Lyn

We dug up Christopher's head*
    and it was rotten —

in this awful place
there is a stinking white canker —

this morning I dug up my feet
    they were rotten —

the facts of frostbite
white then black then gangrenous —

the facts of a lost race
a black Norwegian flag at the pole —

the facts of Scott
muddled, sentimental and a cranky bastard.

Any sportsman knows his odds.
I'll wake up tomorrow, I don't want to.

Can snow and wind tear you to pieces?
This tent as pathetic as a flogged coolie.

I'm a lame fox. The blizzard, the hounds.
I know my dogs.

* Christopher and the other expedition ponies died and were
  buried as food supplies in a snow depot.

WILSON'S DIARY

for Josie and Ian

Cri de coeur
    is simply
        strength of character
whimpering to itself
    on sea-ice
        that is yielding
            to the spine
                of a killer whale —

the water
    is a palaeontologist's
        paradise,
frozen fossils
    surfacing
        to add nostalgia
        to a century
            that likes defrosting
                extinct things,
the water is quite fascinating
            and will kill you
                damn quick!

When the wind drops
    the sea will come for you
        stiff, shuffling, white
            like an Edgar Allan Poe
            bride

whose hands are cold
   whose memory
      is frightfully good —

Have I made myself perfectly clear?

   Yes sir!!
   Toast, fires, chat
            and fagging
               at Eton

   are behind your resolve
         not to look
               to shiver
               to care

ah, the soul is a plateau
            a plateau
               dignified
                     bare —

not a hymn
         of shameless tears
            flooding out
               the conduits
                  of glistening
                        infatuation

well said!

And no sea snakes
      to taunt us here
nothing twisting
      us about
            with beauty

just this avenue of icebergs
      mauve, pink, gold!
ice crystals
    the sham jewels
      of Purgatory!

Hell's Versailles!
can you cope?

If I come South
      (come South!
      come South!)
it's because
    I've fallen in love
and love
    is a trance,
      a marching order!

Let my heart crack
    like a ship destroyed
      in pack ice

let my soul
    perish
    like a sledger pulling
    across an infinite glacier
let my eyes
    blister
      in the blizzard
        of God.

MRS FERN-SMITH

Shooting crocodiles,
dancing around a black, bloodied bull,
wrestling a leopard for its pelt;
    oh Christ,
        the rush (better than heroin)
    of cruelty to dangerous things —

while I teach History
    to dull-eyed, giggling kids
        in (fresh/stale farts) classrooms;
the quiet, suburban dead-end
    cul-de-sac
of a girl's private school.

Thirty years old
    and my rich, long, red hair
    is a plastic Byronic clubfoot
    is greasy
    is falling out
stuck to me
    like fluffy, old cough-drops
        forgotten deep down a pocket —

I have a gaunt, sick face
but great legs
my arms freckle
    even under the moon,
I wear worn jumpers
    stretched to my bum
right through the foul Sydney summer,
I've never cared what I look like —

I like men/I hate girls —

in 1967 what kind of figure
    can any woman cut?

Behind the wheel
    of my husband's Holden
I talk to myself;
my voice is weedy, a school joke,
the little buggers
have got my phone number
they ring me at home
and anonymously taunt me —

my fractured, fucking voice,
    not like the Borgia gutsy voice
of my books —

or book
just the one
    (my red hair, men, gypsies,
        fighting bulls)
"I was gored, girls"
I've never been the same
    that's why my voice,
        my hands, my manner
            are so ...
                castrati!

Christ, I hate teaching
    fresh/stale farts
    boredom as high
                as a mountain of glassy dung,
and my fragile status
    of writer/ratbag

in the staff-room
    stale perfume/stale smoke
    toothaching prattle —

I hate women;
    a private school is a prison
        fetid as a harem,
and moulders
    like a bowling club
    like a mobile cemetery.

I dream of huge, jungle flowers,
    those with a putrid smell;
like shit, rotting flesh,
        decomposition
        as sharp as a squirt
        of sulphuric acid up the nostrils —

this is beauty,
    dainty with barbed wire,
this is beauty,
    delicate in the wind as a gibbet,
I dream of a reeking garden,
I dream of my noxious frailty
    as a flower,
        a jungle flower —

and let the girls
    shriek at my voice and clothes,
let the old bitches on the staff
think I'm a drug addict
    because I won't expose my arms,
let my husband
    hanker after more ordinary women,
I'm a flower

a wild, hidden, foul
   jungle flower

just get a whiff
just get close enough ...

Can I live
   in my own poisonous fumes?
Don't tell me
      I haven't got the guts!
Once
   I wound up the windows
      of my car
and just sat quietly
         just breathed in.

I'm still there.

THE TWINS

*This poem is based on a true story. Jean and Janice are
twins. They choose to talk to no one but each other.
They used to write diaries, poetry and stories together.
The twins are now confined separately in a British
psychiatric hospital.*

Jean's Diary   December

I watch
    the trees in winter;
or do I only watch
    one tree, this tree.
Look at it now.
It's stuck here too
    but is fierce
        against a pale winter sky.
It loves the cold
    it gorges on frost and wind
        to make it black and sharp
            to make it strong.
Beautiful as a stiff thorn
I pass my hand over it
    carefully
as if it were a candle flame
as if it were you, my twin.

Janice's Diary   December

I won't write to you.

No-one can make me.
Not even you.

I won't talk to you.
No-one can make me.
Not even you.

I won't touch your hand.
No-one can make me.
Not even you.

Lithium. Lithium. Lithium.
Ha. Ha. It doesn't work.
I'm fucking dangerous.

I'm watching your Xmas card
burn, my twin.

Jean's Diary   April

Everyone's out in the garden.
They're far away
but their voices are
very close.

I'm looking at the sky
it's our kind of sky, my twin.
No-one could smudge it.
No dirty voice scrapes along it.
It's a closed mouth.
All silent blue
not deep
the smooth insides of a circle
all silent blue.

It's Spring.
You wouldn't care —
            but it's so warm today
            and you'd know this sky.

Janice's Diary   April

Spring.
And I want to burn
    all the places I can't go —

The streets, the parks, the pubs,
my wild bed
that magic place between a man's legs
our room, my twin —

in here the air is damp and cool
but my tongue, my matches
    are dry.

Jean's Diary   May

Remember that room.

Picking up blokes
bringing them back
screwing without chatter.

When it got boring
we started our books.

Diaries. Poems and stories.
Christ, what a lark!

Your leaking biro. Your trembling hand.

Words all over the bed
  all over the floor.

Once you tore it all up
  you wanted to write better

now, my twin,
  you remember that room
    as all talk.

Jean's Diary May

Lights out.
My watch is in the dark.
I can hear it
  tick, my twin.

Is it you?
Are you talking to me?

My throat is dry.
  Water.
  My glass of water.

I miss you.
  Tick. Tick.
    Talk to me.

Jean's Diary 24th June

They told me
I can see you today.

I'm frightened.

My tongue is picking out words
    with care
as if I were picking you out
    an engagement ring.

Please marry me.

The Visit   24th June   Jean

Weak tea and sweet biscuits.

Yes. I've noticed too.
Let's talk
    about something else.

A month.
Count the silent hours
    In a month, my twin.

Your rusty voice
    slags
at the weak tea
    and sweet biscuits.

The Visit   24th June   Janice

I wish you weren't me.

I want someone different,
    my twin.

Your eyes. Your hair.
Repulsive. Intimate as toilet paper.

Even when you're silent
your talk is my talk.

Shut up.

The Visit   24th June   Janice

Today
I am Bluebeard's room
and none of your keys
    fit.

This is not a dare.

Don't kiss me.
Don't snivel. Don't talk.

See you next month.

The Visit   24th June   Jean

Watching you
I'm sick of my own reflection —

I'd like to be a vampire
with no mirror, no twin,
then I wouldn't feed off
    my own flesh
      and starve —

See you next month.

DECEMBER/HOBART

Hobart limps
    with a leg iron
    with the droop of a hunter's rifle
    with the sealer's
    with the convict's sperm
        in the cunt of this tropical stranger
           shivering in this thin thin summer sun,
      holding up the unfamiliar sky
        the cool days
     with smooth, kissed hands
        smudgy eyes
        nothing tells me nothing
I make endless love —

I look at the stars
   from a cramped backyard
overwhelming
   with its smell of chopped wood
     and fresh, new fence;
   the stars are the stars,
I long for a loving, silly voice
      on a public phone —

I'm distracting myself
I'm trying to listen underneath things,
the sparrows in the Botanical Gardens,
the shuffling cold wind
     coming off the dark water, the dark land,
this concrete under my chair
    just as cracked, as respectable,
      as my relatives,

      filling up with the snuff of dead twigs,
the centre of Hobart
where a blues band pricks me
  with a pert harmonica —

I'm trying to hear the Black Drive of 1830;
but hear instead the rattle of pneumonia
and the bedside voice of white Christianity
   plumping the barren pillows
     in graves on Flinders Island;
a clear blue sky
as bland as a revised hymn book
the wind loutish
    throwing things about
    pulling the pinball knobs of the nasty English shrubs,
    really deaf, ignorant,
    it's young and can't remember —

the concrete in its fat silence
  probably knows more
    but is lobotomised with content
      just holding down the dirt
        of this couldn't-swing-a-dead-cat backyard,
those Aborigines
    fat and ugly
      in Christianity's clothes
are much noisier,
I can hear them
  they're like kids
    and make slack servants,
      when they die
        anthropologists souvenir their skulls —

the song of fire
the story of the speared star women

the mutton birds
   dragged screaming from their holes;
this afternoon blowing my pages around
   with the washing
      making gentle shadows on the concrete —

in the State Library
I read about Truganini's
   mysterious love for white man
and how on Flinders Island
   her own people
      addicted to flour, sugar, tea
         and shivering in blankets,
            cursed her;
young Truganini
   stinking of grease and untreated venereal disease
with flash brown eyes
   always running away from home
noisy, tiny, naked;
sharing a blanket with Robinson
as they explored the West Coast
   coaxing the miniscule, but terrifying, tribes
      into boats, into clothes,
      into drink and piety
      into sterility
         and dying in bunches
            or one by quick one —

Truganini, old and shrunken,
      bearded, protected
         and stared at;
before she died
   she pleaded for peace in the grave,
don't let them take my head
or my hands or my feet

not like what they did to my man, King Billy;
what did the university body snatchers
    talk about as they stripped Truganini
        to the bones?
probably cutting and slicing
they muttered
        where do we come from?
        where do we come from?
    science will murder to find out —

I walked along the beach front
        along the murky lapping water,
the sea-gulls were quiet
      and joyless
        huddled in the cold sand;
sometimes I hate this place
    with its damp depression
    and concrete-slab yacht clubs
    designed tight and square
      like hygienic toilet blocks;
I'm living with a man
    cheerful, blond, modern
who swims laps in a chlorinated pool
    and likes champagne
      and the politics of a small bureaucracy
        for lunch —
he giggles, chats, laughs
    and hums his own songs,
between us
      there is no sympathy
        just long talks, restaurant food
        and light understanding;
there is not enough feeling in me
    to romanticise our estrangement
instead I read books

live backwards
imagine Robinson making love to Truganini
for the first time
chuckling with pride,
ah, this beautiful, dirty, black princess!
the man in Christ must have had
his carnal moments!

my god, to learn her language
to dance naked her dances
to carve circles on each other's thighs!
what a lucky day for her
what a lucky day for my diary!
to crash through the bush
to tame a thylacine bitch pup
to shoot roos
and see my wife's dear face
in my morning prayers
[oh, sweet Lord, let her stay in Hobart-town!]
Truganini, Truganini,
words and my own God
they fail me —

three o'clock in the afternoon;
a stranded dark time
like an island penal settlement
watching for sails
on the stained, cold water
of Macquarie Harbour,
and like a convict
serving natural life
I dream of escape
I imagine the wet, giant ferns
as shelter, as food,
then I roast the hearts and livers

of my murdered companions
   on a mean, green-sticked fire
   which smokes acidly into my frozen eyes,
I'm Pierce
I'm Brady
I'm the flogged convict
   who preferred the gallows to the cat;
the tasteless trees, the invisible animals, the rain,
are the knots
   in my lash —

three o'clock in the afternoon;
no, it's not anymore
   time brings back the bush
     and blasts the island
        to grey scrub and brick ruins,
does it still hurt?
I'm in the cold, brown current
I'm under a capsized boat
I'm in leg-irons
   swallow water, swallow water,
        drown quick
I can't, my ankles sting
       then crack
the water tastes awful —

half-past three
old sketches, old photographs
old skill, old carefulness,
my biro's ink will fade
   be sentimental
   be a tourist trap;
that scrawl!
that girl's ravings!
empty head, hollow hand.

II · 'A GIRL MAD AS BIRDS'*

* from 'Love in the Asylum', Dylan Thomas

THE NEW SUPERNOVA

for Judy Beveridge

A royal spoonbill wades
in the fading light
of a new supernova —

the giant star spasms
its spent fuel
into an elongating swamp
that flows and sparkles
around the spoonbill's feet —

the bird's black bill
dips in the shallow light
and feeds gently
off the dying star.

CLIFF-EDGE SPRING

Waratahs
straggle
      in the cliff-edge bush
some have green knots
     when will they unravel
       into dark red
         pluckable beauties?

The golden whistler
     has slate-grey chic
      and a big Minoan eye
she shimmies to her golden mate's
     song

while
     this foot
      sweating in itchy wool
       tired and stupid
        stumbles
         over a purple bush orchid

missing it
     with a wild flower's luck.

'A GIRL MAD AS BIRDS'

Shellshock
        of king parrots
their bright bellies
my hands on a hot stove
the hands I love with

magpies
        tangled dangerously above my head
gurgling like fresh rivers
primary colours
their black and white
        strutting like lovers' chess

lorikeets
        sashay across the balcony
        are always starving
don't feed them sugar
        give it to me instead.

LYING AWAKE AT DAWN

Was it a cackle of kookaburras
        that woke me up?

Or a long lightening shadow
        with pink claws.

Exhausted,
        yet lying awake,
I watch the light arrive
        mangled as a cat's mouse.

Shadows become things,
        the rain wobbles them.
I try closing my eyes.

The rain. The rain.
The grey light picks out
    a touch fastidiously
        grey washing
            getting soaked and heavy on the line.

How does a magpie sing like that?
Its notes always sound like water,
        gurgling mountain water
        wet dawn moonshine
        thrilling as the Devil's fiddle.

Can I play the day
        like Paganini?

THE LAZY POEM

Writing poetry
is for the indolent.

I tell my friends
I work in my head —
That's a lie.

What's the truth?
Well,
    quarter of an hour ago
I idly looked out the window
while pouring steaming water
onto stains of instant coffee
and I saw
in the distinct but cool
late afternoon light
    a crimson rosella
        indecisive
            near a mucky pool
                under a blossoming
                    apple tree.
I liked the rosella's waddle
and red and blue
under white of flowers.

It made
    some kind of
        sticky moment-picture
            that was very lovely.

I'll write a poem
    about it

I thought
    stirring in the sugar.

This is it.

THE SATIN BOWER BIRD

Instead of picking at myself
like an old scab
I'm going to build a bower
and litter it with bits of blue —

you walk towards me
down a Coles aisle
and walk a cute crooked line
like a peroxided Chandler drunk
you're wearing blue
and I want to fly off with you
like a bower bird snitching a bright
blue plastic peg —

under the ripe white moon
looming in broad daylight
flashing all its deep craters
I am pulled like the sea
and feel quite washed up
until
you touch my face
with your fine right hand
and I see it glitter
like a carved Minoan
blue octopus gem stone
and I'm going to sever it
if you leave it lying about
and fix it with bluetack
to my bower wall,
I want to keep it.

I'm not up to my bower dance
but I have other weapons
of seduction,
watch my face
I'll hold my breath
until I turn blue
see?
didn't I always say
I'd die for you.

HAWKESBURY RIVER

The light over the Hawkesbury River
   has been clawed at —

it's a dismal warder of a river
   winding around
      its sandstone cells
      its mangrove pits
         like grey hair —

there's damp breath
   wet hands
      wild thumb-prints
         behind its quiet, conning noon
there's screaming
      at night
      toad-hopping over the water
there's a face
      under a berserk speed boat
         its nose slashed away
            by a frothing blade
there's a child
      in an asylum
      with colourless, pin-prick eyes
         and no name
      who eats shit
   and masturbates
      with a mindless hand
your neighbour
      lives behind heavy curtains
      watching television in the dark

chain-smoking and screaming
   at the corpses of her children
who gobbled oleander pies and chips
while a goat gone wild
   scavenges
      in the bush
      and licks salt
         off the rocks —

I can hear someone
   blubbering
      on the hot wind
someone
   watching their freedom
      burn to ash
on islands
   of grey sand, grey gum
on islands
   of institutional chimneys
islands
   of mouths
      wheezing under concrete
         unmarked graves —

bad, bad dreaming
a history
   of boats
rotting at their moorings
with sharks
   flashing about
      like pimps in a slum —

filthy mattresses
   rise to the surface
      on a claustrophobic cruise

and the launch
      becomes a furiously hot island
with drunken sunstroke
      following you around
         sobbing, vomiting,
           seeing things —

you talk, talk
      in your sleep
to something violating the peace
      with kerosene
         thrashing in the water —

relax,
      it's only the Hawkesbury
      holding a match
         to its heart
      trembling, desolate
         drenched in fumes
wanting futilely
      to go up
      like a giant burning monk.

PICKING UP SHELLEY FROM SCHOOL

for Shelley

Waiting for Shelley
   I always see first
      a kid
         who is not Shelley —

she has pale blow-away legs
a long adult face
      and carries wearily a violin case;
her mother drives up
   almost onto the footpath
      in a dark, expensive car,
relieved, the kid
      skinny leg quickly after skinny leg
         disappears —

then
         after some time
            comes Shelley
               exotic as a rainforest frog,
         she reminds me
            immediately
               it's ice-cream day.

FLESH AND BLOOD

Before you go in you see a flash of lorikeets,
you tell yourself to hang onto it —

when she opens the door
she won't smile at you
but you turn to pity instead of humiliation
and notice her swollen hands, her thin hair,
your old enemy, your father calls her,
she's old all right, she's falling to bits —

the house still has the smell you remember
when you stayed in your room
threaded to your transistor,
if she came in she never knocked —

the toilet is a paranoid closet
no peace in there
you use it again after all these years
and still get anxious
        waiting for her to barge in,
but she can't move now
she's so old, so miserable —

in every room you can hear her painful shuffle
        her heavy breath,
she's everywhere like the carpet smell
but now your heart twists for her
        in a way that's not love or affection;
it's
        she's suffering
        she's flesh and blood

she's you with no imagination
her large, manipulative eyes are yours —

to your surprise, perhaps hers,
she wants you to stay longer
and you stare through the closed window
        at her meticulous garden
                yearning to leave —

when you go she still won't kiss you
        her mouth sour,
your foot trembles on the clutch
        in a sort of grief,
you still hate her suburb
        as you drive away,
it's all white like a leper's spots
you can't get out of it fast enough.

THE RED SPORTS CAR AFTERNOON

In this kind
    of weather,
that reminds me
    far too much
    of apple blossom
and holidays in
    the mountains
as a kid,
I am without garters
    without rules —

even a laundromat
in the freezing cold
can be romantic
when a new place
    is just a movie,
you don't mind pestering the locals
    for a match
or talking too loudly,
    imagining yerself
in a turtle-neck sweater
    narrow eyed
    in black'n'white.

Then a blond
    in a red sports car
falls for you
    and you for him
because in 16 millimetre
    you can't lose —

he says he's married
      nonchalantly
before you start kissing
but to yourself
you're even more two-dimensional
      than his wife

so you snatch at
      his mouth, hands
      and armfuls of
      bizarre affection
and stand under trees
      under lights
      on the beach
and think up
incoherent lines neat.

Wow.
We say together.
How did this happen?
and *Are you all right?*
I feel confused
We'll think it over
      tonight —

me sleeping
      in the bower bird's
      nest
of a stranger's blue books
you with yer wife.

C'est la vie.
I must have said.
It's aspros with coke
      for when the

      house lights
go up
     hissing
like an all-night train sludge
    of relatives
       and morality.

One way
   or another
I'm gonna find ya
I'm gonna getcha
        getcha —

the beauty of rock music
its sexual
    optimism
every record collection
    collects groupies
    collects dust
    collects people on
      holiday
where every second
    is a silver plane
and showing off
    to the hosties
I'm from Sydney Megalopolis!
    and I work
    for *The Daily Planet*
and all I want
    is a married man —

I will give you
    my finest hour
the one I spent
    watching you shower

his wife singing
    in the carburettor
of a red sports car —

freezing cold weather

our commercial
    has goose-bumps
this movie
    is kero-
blue and fantastic

a line I've used
    in another poem
about snow
about happiness
about an Alpine ad
now
    blue'n' fantastic

I smell kero
I can see me
    setting you
        on fire
and it working too —
I mean a wedding
    celebrant
quoting 'Desiderata'
    in a heat wave —

and *now*
    it's a red sports car
      roaring
like the inside of a pistol
and a poetry reading
    when a blond

followed me
    home
        like a fall of glittering snow
in a Russell Drysdale
    Xmas card
        and drove me off
in a red sports car that was
    double-jointed.

WHEN DESIRE'S GONE

I

It's not necessarily
   a long blank night
when desire's gone —

there's still old love
   hanging around
like a forgotten dressing gown

there's still television
   favourite meals
and chat and memory —

when desire's gone.

But
   you reach for a book
instead of your lover's hand

your mood is cosy
   not tremulous,
your sleep is dry and dusty

and the stars
   are the pattern
      on a tea-towel —

when desire's gone.

II

The dance   King David remembers the dance
dancing before the ark   before God
feet   ecstasy   nakedness
dancing before God   the ark gold
moving towards him swarming terrifying
like a plague of burning locusts
this dance before God   dancing before God
I remember   I remember
geriatric David freezing
crawling over the ribs of his teenage concubine
can't dance   can't feel the storm of God in his blood
thorns of dust through the feet
can't desire   can't dance before God.

III

A blue winged horse
    in a provincial zoo;
clipped, gelded,
wired in, sides and roof
        like a chookhouse;
a fouled, cement floor —

it's blue
like a dark, deep sea
        against black shore cliffs
        at high voltage summer noon;
but the horse
        stands like an abandoned
            mare
        in a knacker's yard,
eyes as blunt
        as a junkie's.

Someone's pet maybe.

No longer a cute foal
        flying around the house
        sniffing and sneezing
        in the dusty corners
            of ceilings —

got too big,
            too wild to fly
or perhaps
        turned vicious
and couldn't be trusted.

IV

I still have the skeleton key
    to a house
        that's been torn down —

I can still smell it;
    but can no longer run my life
        along its sharp corners,
no longer dream
        in its sea-garden —

I write the house dead letters;
letters
        blown up like condom balloons
letters
        rotten with termites
letters
        whipped along in the cold, dirty wind
        like chucked-out junk mail —

no telephone
no street number

just a precipice of home units
above
      a stalled, iron-grey glacier.

III · THE AMULET

Wild Nights — Wild Nights!
Were I with thee
Wild Nights should be
Our Luxury!

Emily Dickinson

DRIVING TOO FAST

Driving too fast
I can't wait to see you —

Driving too fast
I'm wet. I'm nuts. too much pop music.

Driving too fast
how tight can you hold me?

Driving too fast
be a tiger shark. maul my mouth.

Driving too fast
your eyes are sulky   different   wonderful. taste strange.

Driving too fast
be by yourself. be randy.

Driving too fast
let the car break down tomorrow.

Driving too fast
it's your street. it's Alpha Centauri.

Driving too fast
hand brake. stillness.

YOUR KISSES

Smashed glass;
I flirt on shining cut feet.

Your mouth is cut glass
not decanter, not wine stem, what?

I cut myself into delirious shards;
the light shines like a wild fly's eye.

Then smashes;
a panting, pinned fly.

Hold this full glass to the light
kiss it smashed.

STRAWBERRIES SONNET

You're all bones
You're all quicksilver skin
Rough as a wild night
You're not strawberries.
Your hands are ice
Your tongue cuts my face
Into conquered turf
You're not strawberries.
You're a determined wasp
Dying on my sting
You're my murder and my delight
You're not strawberries.

Your fingers play my windpipe
You're not strawberries.

LOLLIES NOIR

And the telephone comes to mean
    something awesome to us
just like
    those taut stale symbols
       in horror films —

in a kind of heavy-strings suspense
    I ring you
and my heart *hurts*
    as if it were thrilling
       to a beautiful clichéd wound —

I want you
    to creep up on me;
to jam my Sunday School's party line
    with heavy breathing —

and it's that psychopathic step
    on the stair
that makes me sober
    makes me aware —

in *naked terror*
    there's a blurb of stillness
transcending
    bad acting
    cheap sets
    lukewarm love

there's waiting for death
there's shooting someone in the head

there's taking you
    cruelly
by the spines
      to find out
      what you really said —
but it's the dream
      of you
    in a black ballet
that really turns me on —

that little *c'est impossible, ma cherie* —

Cobra Lake!

DRIVING HOME AT 3 A.M.

Window open
radio on, sweet prickles of pop music,
warm dazed night
I'm exhilarated, exhausted
shouldn't be driving
should have stayed sleeping

an arm, an exhausted arm,
hooked around you in a single bed.

WUNJO*

Tonight
        my room is different,
                miraculous
I leave it
come back to it,
you're still in my bed —

you're smoking
you're propped up on my pillows
your naked skin pale   dark   lovely
        in the light
                of my rickety reading lamp —

what have you looked at
        while I've been gone?
my shelves of books, my messy desk
        my glass of water ...

* The rune of joy

PMT

The moon is out this morning.
Full,
    and the yellow
      of old dentures.
Nothing like a moon
    in a fastidious T'ang poem
it stares through
    the mist, the traffic, my windscreen,
like a mesmerising chilblain.

The radio is a box of Fantales;
    gossip, rubbish
      and caramel.
I chew on it
thinking about
    my long weekend
    my lover's delectable mouth.
But the moonlight
    splashes on my driving hands
      like freezing water
and I count my jerky heart-beats
    backwards.

CARS. LIGHTNING. RAIN.

Cars. Lightning. Rain.
Your cheek on my hair.
Strawberries. White wine.
A mess in the back seat.

I drive you home
and we chat between thunder claps
about the fall of Crete.

A bare-breasted goddess
at ease, insouciant control,
holding firmly with feminine hands
two writhing snakes.

Secretly
        I imagine loving you
            like that,
my feet balanced
            apart,
hanging on without fear
            to any pet reptile between us.

But between kisses
        my breath tears like wet paper,
holding you in my arms
        is a tender farce or a blubbering High Mass;
        I skid on my wrenched heart
            even more than this old car
                skids on the drenched road.

Cars. Lightning. Rain.

When you leave me
I watch every Minoan fresco
        ever painted and cherished
            drip and burn.

THE AMULET

Is love as ruthless as death?

You lie,
        faintly awkward,
            in my lap
and I marvel
            at your fine, perishable face.
I trace it
        with my thrilled fingers
and feel
            the faintly damp
            living heat of your skin.

Eyes. Hair-line. Bones. Nose. Mouth.
I feel
        that futile gloat of possession
like wanting to be buried
        with your gold.
You are not mine.
I am not yours.
We don't even own ourselves.
Soul, heart, blood
        each other
    our sapphire world
    all on unreliable loan.

Our love stabs so deep
I'm amazed the cuts
can't fountain a power
to fight death
        to the death.

My mouth quietly on yours
my pulse purposefully calm
so I can hear
    the strange closeness
        of your heart-beat,
I am in a paradise lagoon
    of the present tense
my life swims with your life
we dive in each other's blood.

I hold this experience
    against my own mortality.
I hold it to us
    like an ice-hot amulet
        of pain and magic.
      Let's go.

ACKNOWLEDGEMENTS

Some of these poems were first published in the Australian, the Australian Literary Supplement, Blue Light Lounge, Helix, Overland, The Penguin Book of Australian Women Poets, Phoenix Review, New Poetry, Simply Living, the Sydney Morning Herald, Westerly, Women Australia, Writers in the Park — the Book, and Kiwi and Emu; others have been broadcast by ABC radio (The Coming Out Show) and 2SER (The Humanities Hour): I am grateful to their editors and producers.

COPYRIGHT

ligature *un*tapped

This print edition published in collaboration with Brio Books,
an imprint of Booktopia Group Ltd

Level 6, 1A Homebush Bay Drive · Rhodes NSW 2138 · Australia

Print ISBN: 9781761281013

briobooks.com.au

MIX
Paper from
responsible sources
FSC® C008194

The paper in this book is FSC® certified.
FSC® promotes environmentally responsible,
socially beneficial and economically viable
management of the world's forests.